NORTH DAKOTA

States

by Tyler Maine

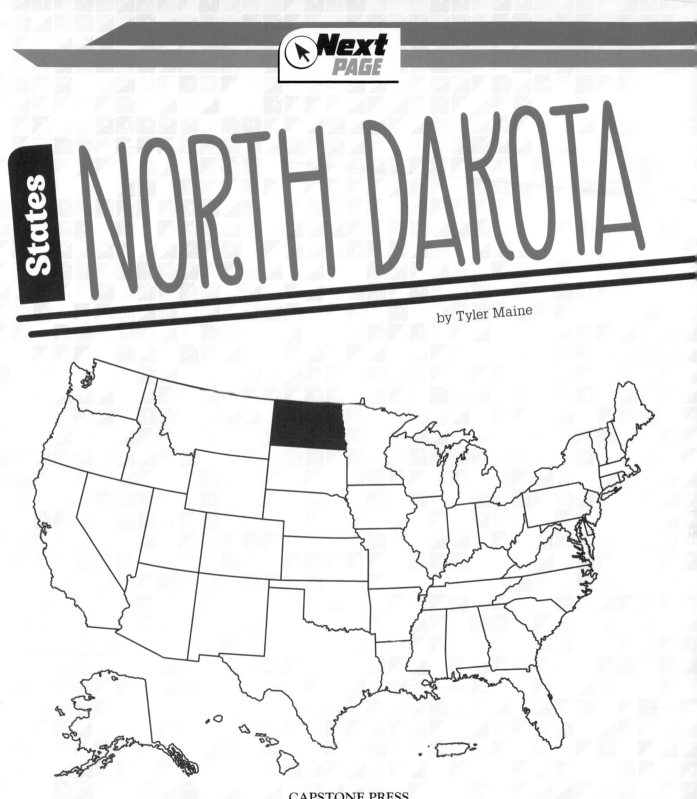

CAPSTONE PRESS
a capstone imprint

Next Page Books are published by Capstone Press,
1710 Roe Crest Drive, North Mankato, Minnesota 56003
www.mycapstone.com

Library of Congress Cataloging-in-Publication Data
Cataloging-in-publication information is on file with the Library of
Congress.
ISBN 978-1-5157-0421-8 (library binding)
ISBN 978-1-5157-0480-5 (paperback)
ISBN 978-1-5157-0532-1 (ebook PDF)

Editorial Credits
Jaclyn Jaycox, editor; Richard Korab and Katy LaVigne, designers;
Morgan Walters, media researcher; Tori Abraham, production specialist

Photo Credits
Capstone Press: Angi Gahler, map 4, 7; Dreamstime: Igor Voronchikhin,
9, Sakkawokkie, 17; Getty Images: Archive Photos/MPI, middle 19,
Danita Delimont, 11, Getty Images Entertainment/Ulf Andersen, top
18, Michael Ochs Archives, bottom 19; iStockphoto: jerryhopman, 5;
Library of Congress: Prints and Photographs Division/Geo. Prince,
top 19, 25; Newscom: Andre Jenny Stock Connection Worldwide, 10;
North Wind Picture Archives, 12, 27; One Mile Up, Inc., flag, seal 23;
Shutterstock: Ace Diamond, 13, Artens, bottom right 8, Blulz60, bottom
right 21, Deyan Georgiev, top 24, Don Mammoser, top right 21, Everett
Historical, 26, FiledIMAGE, bottom left 8, Jay Stuhlmiller, top right
20, John Huntington, 29, Kletr, bottom right 20, Merkushev Vasiliy,
middle left 21, PhotoStock10, 15, RRuntsch, cover, 7, s_bukley, middle
18, salajean, bottom 24, Singkham, 14, Steve Oehlenschlager, 16, Tom
Reichner, bottom left 20, Tyler Hartl, bottom left 21, ver0nicka, 17,
volkovslava, 28; Superstock: Nomad, bottom 18; Wikimedia: Bjr97543,
6, François Marchal, top left 21, Matt Lavin, top left 20, USDA-NRCS
PLANTS Database/Sheri Hagwood, middle right 21

All design elements by Shutterstock

Printed and bound in China.
0316/CA21600187
012016   009436F16

TABLE OF CONTENTS

Want to take your research further? Ask your librarian if your school subscribes to PebbleGo Next. If so, when you see this helpful symbol 🖱 throughout the book, log onto www.pebblegonext.com for bonus downloads and information.

LOCATION

North Dakota is one of the nation's midwestern states. It's located in the north-central United States. To the north are Canada's provinces of Saskatchewan and Manitoba. To the south is South Dakota. Montana lies to the west, and Minnesota is on the east. North Dakota's capital, Bismarck, is on the east bank of the Missouri River. Fargo, Bismarck, Grand Forks, Minot, and Mandan are the state's largest cities.

PebbleGo Next Bonus!
To print and label
your own map, go to
www.pebblegonext.com
and search keywords:
ND MAP

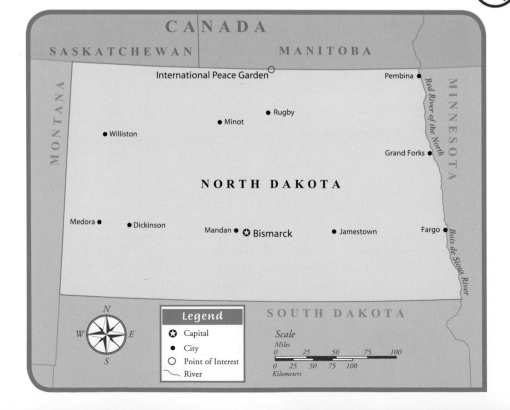

CANADA

SASKATCHEWAN   MANITOBA

International Peace Garden   Pembina ●

MONTANA

● Williston   ● Minot   ● Rugby

Grand Forks ●

Red River of the North

MINNESOTA

NORTH DAKOTA

Medora ●   ● Dickinson   Mandan ● ✪ Bismarck   ● Jamestown   Fargo ●

Bois de Sioux River

N
W ✦ E
S

SOUTH DAKOTA

Legend
✪ Capital
● City
○ Point of Interest
〰 River

Scale
Miles
0   25   50   75   100
0   25   50   75   100
Kilometers

4

Bismarck was founded in 1872 and originally named Edwinton. The city was renamed in 1873.

GEOGRAPHY

North Dakota is part of two land regions. The Central Lowlands cover eastern North Dakota. The Red River Valley, the flattest and lowest area of the state, is found here. The Great Plains cover western North Dakota. The Missouri Coteau, on the eastern edge of the Great Plains, has low rolling hills. The Coteau Slope has slightly higher hills. The Missouri Plateau in the southwest has broad valleys and flat-topped hills called buttes. White Butte is the state's highest point, rising 3,506 feet (1,069 meters) above sea level.

PebbleGo Next Bonus! To watch a video about the Lewis and Clark Interpretive Center, go to www.pebblegonext.com and search keywords:

White Butte gets its chalky white color from the mudstone and claystone its made of.

A large variety of animals live in Theodore Roosevelt National Park, including bison, horses, snakes, and lizards.

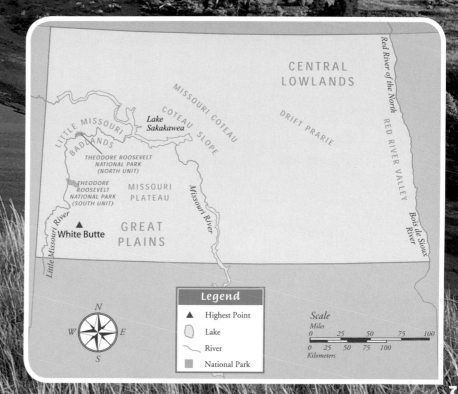

CENTRAL LOWLANDS

MISSOURI COTEAU

COTEAU SLOPE

DRIFT PRARIE

RED RIVER VALLEY

Red River of the North

LITTLE MISSOURI

BADLANDS

Lake Sakakawea

THEODORE ROOSEVELT NATIONAL PARK (NORTH UNIT)

THEODORE ROOSEVELT NATIONAL PARK (SOUTH UNIT)

MISSOURI PLATEAU

Missouri River

Little Missouri River

▲ White Butte

GREAT PLAINS

Bois de Sioux River

Legend

▲ Highest Point

⬠ Lake

〰 River

▢ National Park

Scale
Miles
0 25 50 75 100

0 25 50 75 100
Kilometers

N
W E
S

WEATHER

North Dakota's summers are warm with clear skies, but the winters can be bitterly cold. Winter weather can last from November to April. The average January temperature is 7 degrees Fahrenheit (minus 14 degrees Celsius). In July the average temperature is 70°F (21°C).

Average High and Low Temperatures (Bismarck, ND)

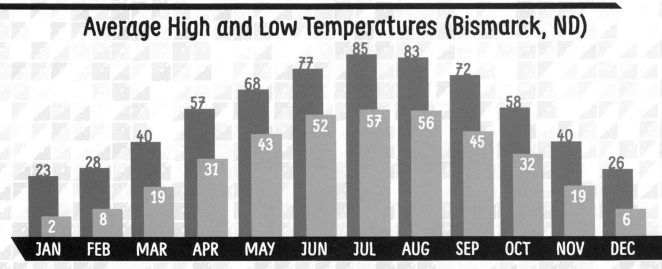

	JAN	FEB	MAR	APR	MAY	JUN	JUL	AUG	SEP	OCT	NOV	DEC
High	23	28	40	57	68	77	85	83	72	58	40	26
Low	2	8	19	31	43	52	57	56	45	32	19	6

Geographical Center of North America

This spot is the north-south and east-west midpoint of the continent. It is located near the city of Rugby in north-central North Dakota.

International Peace Garden

This garden straddles the border between North Dakota and the Canadian province of Manitoba. It gives North Dakota its nickname, the Peace Garden State.

Fort Yates

Famous Hunkpapa Lakota Sioux chief Sitting Bull was buried near Fort Yates, North Dakota. His remains were moved in 1953. A monument now marks the spot of his original burial ground on the Standing Rock Sioux Reservation.

HISTORY AND GOVERNMENT

By the time the first European explored North Dakota, the Mandan Indians had built villages, grown crops, and set up a trading system.

North Dakota's earliest people arrived thousands of years ago. Over time many American Indian groups came to live in North Dakota.

In 1682 René-Robert Cavelier, known as Sieur de La Salle, claimed present-day North Dakota for France. In 1803 the United States bought the land from France as part of the Louisiana Purchase. Dakota Territory was created in 1861. It included most of present-day North Dakota and South Dakota. Settlers and big farming companies began moving in when the Northern Pacific Railroad reached the land in the 1870s. In 1889 North Dakota became the 39th U.S. state.

North Dakota's government has executive, legislative, and judicial branches. The governor is the head of the executive branch. The legislative branch consists of North Dakota's legislative assembly. Its two sections are the 49-member Senate and the 98-member House of Representatives. The judicial branch is made up of judges and their courts.

North Dakota's capitol building is the tallest in the state at 241 feet (73 m).

INDUSTRY

North Dakota is known for its good farmland and large cattle ranches. One of the state's biggest natural resources is its rich, fertile soil. Agriculture has been the most important part of the state's economy since statehood, accounting for roughly 11 percent of North Dakota's economic activity. But agriculture is not the state's only source of income.

Coal mining and oil drilling also help North Dakota's economy. Most of the oil is drilled in the Williston Basin, which is in the western part of the state.

North Dakota's richest soil comes from the Red River Valley.

In recent years the state's medical and financial service industries have helped the state grow as well. Insurance and real estate are also important service industries in North Dakota.

North Dakota is one of the leading oil producers in the United States.

POPULATION

Since the first Mandan Indians settled along the Missouri River, many people have come to North Dakota, and many have left. North Dakota has only about 720,000 people. In recent years, however, North Dakota's population has increased faster than any other U.S. state. People have moved to western North Dakota to work in the oil industry.

People with European backgrounds make up nearly 90 percent of North Dakota's population. American Indians are the second-largest ethnic group in the state. They make up about 5 percent of the population. A small percentage of North Dakota's population is Hispanic, African-American, or Asian.

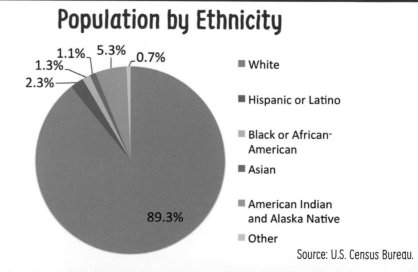

Population by Ethnicity

- 1.1%
- 1.3%
- 2.3%
- 5.3%
- 0.7%
- 89.3%

- ■ White
- ■ Hispanic or Latino
- ■ Black or African-American
- ■ Asian
- ■ American Indian and Alaska Native
- ■ Other

Source: U.S. Census Bureau.

FAMOUS PEOPLE

Louise Erdrich (1954–) is a successful novelist. She grew up in Wahpeton and is a member of the Turtle Mountain Band of Chippewa. Her writing draws on her American Indian and German-American background.

Phil Jackson (1945–) was a successful professional basketball coach until his retirement in 2011. He was a star player for the New York Knicks, coached the Chicago Bulls to six national championships, and coached the Los Angeles Lakers for five years. He grew up in Williston and graduated from the University of North Dakota.

Louis L'Amour (1908–1988) was a writer of western novels. He was born Louis LaMoore in Jamestown.

Theodore Roosevelt (1858–1919) was the 26th U.S. president (1901–1909). He owned ranches in the Badlands near Medora. As president he worked to protect natural lands in the West. He was born in New York City.

Sacagawea (circa 1781–1812) was a Shoshone guide who traveled with the Lewis and Clark expedition. Her name is said to mean "bird woman."

Lawrence Welk (1903–1992) was an accordion player and bandleader. His *Lawrence Welk Show* was a popular TV show in the 1950s. He was born on a farm near Strasburg.

STATE SYMBOLS

Tree
American elm

Flower
wild prairie rose

Bird
western meadowlark

Fish
northern pike

PebbleGo Next Bonus! To make a dessert using a popular North Dakota vegetable, go to www.pebblegonext.com and search keywords:
ND RECIPE

Honorary Equine

Nokota horse

Fruit

chokecherry

Fossil

teredo petrified wood

Grass

western wheatgrass

Insect

convergent lady beetle

Dance

square dance

FAST FACTS

STATEHOOD
1889

CAPITAL ☆
Bismarck

LARGEST CITY •
Fargo

SIZE
60,001 square miles (155,402 square kilometers) land area (2010 U.S. Census Bureau)

POPULATION
723,393 (2013 U.S. Census estimate)

STATE NICKNAME
Peace Garden State

STATE MOTTO
"Liberty and Union, Now and Forever, One and Inseparable"

STATE SEAL

North Dakota's seal was adopted in 1889. It reflects important parts of the state's history. Bundles of wheat, one of the state's main crops, surround an oak tree. The 42 stars over the tree represent the number of states that were part of the nation in 1889. An American Indian hunting buffalo represents the state's native people. The state motto, "Liberty and Union, Now and Forever, One and Inseparable," appears on the seal.

PebbleGo Next Bonus! To print and color your own flag, go to www.pebblegonext.com and search keywords:

ND FLAG

STATE FLAG

The North Dakota flag was adopted in 1911. The flag is blue with an eagle in the center. The eagle stands for strength. It holds an olive branch for peace and arrows for war. Thirteen stars above the eagle stand for the first 13 states. The state name is in a scroll at the bottom.

MINING PRODUCTS

petroleum, coal, natural gas, sand and gravel

MANUFACTURED GOODS

machinery, food products, petroleum and coal products, fabricated metal products, nonmetallic mineral products, wood products

FARM PRODUCTS

wheat, sugar beets, potatoes, soybeans, sunflowers, milk, barley, flaxseed, beef, wool

PebbleGo Next Bonus! To learn the lyrics to the state song, go to www.pebblegonext.com and search keywords:
ND SONG

NORTH DAKOTA TIMELINE

1300s–1600s
Mandan Indians live in the area that is now North Dakota.

1620
The Pilgrims establish a colony in the New World in present-day Massachusetts.

1682
René-Robert Cavelier, Sieur de La Salle, claims land that includes North Dakota for France.

1738
French explorer Pierre La Vérendrye visits Mandan villages in the Missouri River area.

 **1803**

The United States gains southwestern North Dakota in the Louisiana Purchase.

 **1804–1805**

Members of the Lewis and Clark expedition explore North Dakota and spend the winter at Fort Mandan.

 **1818**

Northeastern North Dakota becomes U.S. territory.

 1861

Dakota Territory is created.

1861–1865

The Union and the Confederacy fight the Civil War; the Dakota Territories are under Union President Abraham Lincoln's control, but do not fight on either side of the war.

1880s

Bonanza farms, huge farms owned by investors from other states, become common in the Red River Valley.

1889

North Dakota becomes the 39th U.S. state on November 2.

1914–1918

World War I is fought; the United States enters the war in 1917.

1916

Nonpartisan League candidates, who represent a new political party formed in North Dakota favoring state control of businesses, win elections for almost every state office.

1939–1945

World War II is fought; the United States enters the war in 1941.

 **1951** Oil is discovered near Tioga.

 **1953** Workers finish building the Garrison Dam, which provides hydroelectric power for the state, on the Missouri River.

 **1960** The last power generation unit is installed on the Garrison Dam.

 **1972** The United States makes a deal to sell grain to the Soviet Union, creating good prices for North Dakota farmers.

 **1988** North Dakota suffers a severe drought.

 **1997** The Red River floods, destroying homes and causing the evacuation of Grand Forks.

 **2008** U.S. Geological Survey releases an assessment of undiscovered oil resources in the Bakken Formation, a shale rock formation in western North Dakota.

 **2011** Flooding forces thousands to evacuate Minot and breaks a century-old record for high water.

 **2015** An oil train derails in rural North Dakota in May, causing the cars to start on fire. The nearby town of Heimdal is evacuated.

Glossary

ethnic *(ETH-nik)*—related to a group of people and their culture

executive *(ig-ZE-kyuh-tiv)*—the branch of government that makes sure laws are followed

expedition *(ek-spuh-DI-shuhn)*—a journey with a goal, such as exploring or searching for something

hydroelectric *(hye-droh-i-LEK-trik)*—to do with the production of electricity from moving water

industry *(IN-duh-stree)*—a business which produces a product or provides a service

investor *(in-VEST-uhr)*—someone who provides money for a project in return for a share in the profits

legislature *(LEJ-iss-lay-chur)*—a group of elected officials who have the power to make or change laws for a country or state

novel *(NOV-uhl)*—a book that tells a long story about made-up people and events

petroleum *(puh-TROH-lee-uhm)*—an oily liquid found below the earth's surface used to make gasoline, heating oil, and many other products

ranch *(RANCH)*—a large farm for cattle, sheep, or horses

shale *(SHAYL)*—rock formed from hardened mud

Read More

Bailer, Darice. *What's Great About North Dakota?* Our Great States. Minneapolis: Lerner Publications Company, 2015.

Ganeri, Anita. *United States of America: A Benjamin Blog and His Inquisitive Dog Guide.* Country Guides. Chicago: Heinemann Raintree, 2015.

Sanders, Doug. *North Dakota.* It's My State! New York: Cavendish Square Publishing, 2016.

Internet Sites

FactHound offers a safe, fun way to find Internet sites related to this book. All of the sites on FactHound have been researched by our staff.

Here's all you do:

Visit *www.facthound.com*

Type in this code: 9781515704218

 Check out projects, games and lots more at
www.capstonekids.com

Critical Thinking Using the Common Core

1. What is the geographical center of North America and what city is it located near? (Key Ideas and Details)

2. People with European backgrounds make up what percentage of North Dakota's population? (Key Ideas and Details)

3. Novelist Louise Erdich and writer of western novels Louis L'Amour both grew up in North Dakota. What is a novel? (Craft and Structure)

Index